THE ART OF WEALTH

A Guide To Making Money As An Artist

TABLE OF CONTENTS

Introduction

Chapter 1 - "Understanding the Business of Art"

Chapter 2 - "Developing a Strong Personal Brand"

Chapter 3 - "Finding Your Niche and Target Market"

Chapter 4 - "Pricing Your Artwork Effectively"

Chapter 5 - "Selling Your Art Online"

Chapter 6 - "Marketing Your Art and Building a Following"

Chapter 7 - "Getting Representation and Working with Galleries"

Chapter 8 - "Creating and Selling Art Licenses"

Chapter 9 - "Teaching Art Classes and Workshops"

Chapter 10 - "Collaborating and Networking with Other Artists"

Chapter 11 - "Diversifying Your Income Streams"

Chapter 12 - "Managing Your Finances and Staying Focused on Your Goals"

INTRODUCTION

Welcome to "The Art of Wealth: A Guide to Making Money as an Artist." As an artist, you have a unique talent and passion that sets you apart from the rest. But turning your art into a profitable career can be a challenging and daunting task. That's where this book comes in.

Based on principles proven through decades of application, "The Art of Wealth" is a comprehensive guide that will teach you everything you need to know to turn your art into a profitable career. You'll learn about the various ways that artists can monetize their work, as well as the key factors that influence the value of art. You'll also learn about the importance of building a strong personal brand and understanding your target market.

But "The Art of Wealth" isn't just about making money. It's about building a successful and sustainable career as an artist. You'll learn about the challenges that artists face when trying to make a living from their work, and how to overcome them. You'll also learn about the importance of staying organized and keeping track of your finances as you work to build a successful career.

❋ ❋ ❋

Here are a few details about what you can expect to learn from "The Art of Wealth: A Guide to Making Money as an Artist":

Understanding the business of art: In this chapter, you'll learn about the various ways that artists can monetize their work, including selling original artwork, licensing their artwork, teaching art classes and workshops, collaborating with other artists, and diversifying their income streams. You'll also learn about the key factors that influence the value of art, including the quality and uniqueness of the work, the artist's reputation and track record, and the demand for the artist's work.

Developing a strong personal brand: Your personal brand is the unique combination of your skills, experience, personality, and values that sets you apart from other artists. In this chapter, you'll learn about the importance of developing a strong personal brand and how to do so. You'll also learn about the role that your personal brand plays in attracting potential buyers and building a loyal following.

Finding your niche and target market: In this chapter, you'll learn about the importance of finding your niche and target market as an artist. You'll learn how to identify the specific group of people who are most likely to be interested in your art, and how to tailor your marketing and sales efforts to reach them effectively.

Pricing your artwork effectively: You'll learn about the various factors that go into pricing your artwork effectively, including the cost of materials, framing, and shipping. You'll also learn about strategies for setting your prices and how to negotiate with potential buyers.

Selling your art online: The internet has opened up new opportunities for artists to sell their work directly to buyers. In this chapter, you'll learn about the various online platforms and marketplaces that artists can use to sell their art, as well as best practices for marketing and selling your art online.

Marketing your art and building a following: In this chapter, you'll learn about the various marketing strategies and tactics that you can use to promote your art and build a loyal following. You'll learn about the importance of social media, email marketing, and in-person events, as well as how to create and implement an effective marketing plan.

So if you're ready to turn your art into a profitable career, grab your copy of "The Art of Wealth" and let's get started!

CHAPTER 1

Understanding the Business of Art

Understanding the Business of Art is a crucial chapter for any artist looking to make a living from their work. In this chapter, you'll learn about the various ways that artists can monetize their art, as well as the key factors that influence the value of art. You'll also learn about the importance of building a strong personal brand and understanding your target market. Additionally, you'll learn about the various challenges that artists face when trying to make a living from their work, including the importance of pricing your artwork effectively and finding ways to sell your art online. Finally, you'll learn about the importance of staying organized and keeping track of your finances as you work to build a successful career as an artist.

There are many different ways that artists can monetize their work, and it's important to understand all of the different options available to you as you work to build a successful career. Some common ways that artists make money include:

Selling original artwork: This is perhaps the most obvious way for artists to monetize their work. You can sell your original artwork through galleries, art fairs, online marketplaces, or directly to collectors.

Licensing your artwork: Another way for artists to make money is by licensing their artwork for use in commercial projects. This could include things like book covers, album art, or promotional materials.

Teaching art classes and workshops: Many artists also make money by teaching art classes or workshops. This can be a great way to share your skills and knowledge with others while also earning an income.

Collaborating with other artists: Collaborating with other artists can be a great way to expand your reach and build a bigger audience. You can collaborate on art projects, exhibitions, or other creative ventures.

Diversifying your income streams: Finally, it's important to diversify your income streams as an artist. This means finding multiple ways to monetize your work, rather than relying on just one stream of income. This can help to increase your overall financial stability and reduce your risk of financial instability.

As you can see, there are many different ways for artists to make money from their work. By understanding the business of art and the various monetization strategies available to you, you'll be well-equipped to build a successful and sustainable career as an artist.

Selling original artwork is one of the most common ways for artists to monetize their work. When selling original artwork, there are a few key considerations to keep in mind:

1. Pricing: It's important to have a clear understanding of the value of your work when pricing your artwork. The value of art is influenced by many factors, including the quality and uniqueness of the work, the artist's reputation and track record, and the demand for the artist's work. You'll also need to consider the cost of materials, framing, and shipping when pricing your artwork. When pricing your artwork, it's important to have a clear understanding of the value of your work. There are a few factors to consider when determining the value of your artwork:

   - Quality and uniqueness: The quality and uniqueness of your work will be a key factor in determining its value. High-quality artwork that is well-crafted and original will typically command a higher price than lower-quality or more generic work.
   - Reputation and track record: The reputation and track record of the artist can also influence the value of the artwork. Artists with a strong reputation and a proven track record of selling their work will typically be able to command higher prices for their artwork.
   - Demand: Finally, the demand for your work will also play a role in determining its value. If there is high demand for your work, you'll be able to command higher prices for your artwork.

2. Marketing: To sell your original artwork, you'll need to effectively market your work to potential buyers. This

can be done through a variety of channels, including social media, email marketing, and in-person events like art fairs and exhibitions. Marketing: To sell your original artwork, you'll need to effectively market your work to potential buyers. There are many different ways to market your artwork, including:

- Social media: Social media platforms like Instagram, Facebook, and Twitter can be effective ways to promote your artwork and reach a wider audience.
- Email marketing: Email marketing can be a powerful way to reach potential buyers directly and build a relationship with them over time.
- In-person events: In-person events like art fairs, exhibitions, and open studios can be a great way to connect with potential buyers and showcase your work.

3. Sales channels: There are many different channels through which you can sell your original artwork. These include galleries, art fairs, online marketplaces, and directly to collectors. Each channel has its own pros and cons, so it's important to carefully consider which channels are the best fit for your work and target market. Some common options include:

- Galleries: You can sell your original artwork through galleries, either on a consignment basis or by negotiating a direct sale. There are four main types of art galleries: commercial, mega, vanity, and exhibition spaces. Commercial galleries represent and support artists, selling their artwork and earning a commission. Mega galleries are highly influential and have multiple locations, representing only the best artists and advising institutions and events in the art world. Vanity galleries charge artists to exhibit and promote their work, and are not known for having a good reputation or selection of artists based on quality. Exhibition spaces are rented by artists to organize their own exhibitions, and are not curated by a gallery owner. Public galleries are funded by the government and showcase a variety of artwork, while nonprofit galleries focus on supporting emerging artists and promoting a specific cause or theme.

- Art fairs: Art fairs can be a great way to showcase your work to a wider audience and make sales directly to buyers.
- Online marketplaces: There are many online marketplaces that allow artists to sell their original artwork directly to buyers. Some popular options include Saatchi Art, Etsy, and Society6.
- Direct to collectors: Finally, you can sell your artwork directly to collectors by reaching out to them directly or through your personal network.

4. Negotiating and closing sales: When selling your original artwork, you may need to negotiate with potential buyers to reach an agreement on the terms of the sale. This can include things like the price, payment terms, and delivery or shipping details. It's important to be clear and professional when negotiating with buyers, and to make sure that all terms of the sale are clearly documented in writing. When selling your original artwork, you may need to negotiate with potential buyers to reach an agreement on the terms of the sale. This can include things like the price, payment terms, and delivery or shipping details. It's important to be clear and professional when negotiating with buyers, and to make sure that all terms of the sale are clearly documented in writing.

By understanding these key considerations, you'll be well-equipped to sell your original artwork and build a successful career as an artist.

※ ※ ※

Licensing your artwork is another way for artists to monetize their work. When you license your artwork, you allow others to use it for specific purposes in exchange for a fee. Some common ways that artists license their artwork include:

1. Commercial use: You can license your artwork for use in commercial projects, such as book covers, album art, or promotional materials. In these cases, the licensee (the party using the artwork) will typically pay a fee to use the artwork for a specific purpose and time period. When licensing your artwork for commercial use, it's important to have a clear understanding of the terms of the license agreement. This typically includes things like the duration of the license, the rights being granted (e.g., exclusive or non-exclusive), and the fees being paid to the artist. You'll also need to consider the specific purpose for which the artwork will be used and how it will be reproduced. For example, if your artwork is being used on a book cover, you'll need to consider things like the size of the artwork, the printing process, and whether it will be used in print or digital formats.

2. Merchandise: You can also license your artwork for use on merchandise, such as t-shirts, mugs, or other products. In these cases, the licensee will typically pay a royalty on each item sold. When licensing your artwork

for use on merchandise, you'll typically receive a royalty on each item sold. The amount of the royalty will depend on the terms of the license agreement, as well as the price of the merchandise. It's important to carefully consider the terms of the license agreement and make sure that you are being fairly compensated for the use of your artwork.

3. Print-on-demand services: Some artists use print-on-demand services like Society6 or Redbubble to license their artwork for use on a wide range of products. These services allow you to upload your artwork and choose which products you'd like it to be available on. Whenever someone orders a product with your artwork on it, the service will print and ship the product to the customer.

To license your artwork, you'll need to have a clear understanding of the terms of the license agreement. This typically includes things like the duration of the license, the rights being granted (e.g., exclusive or non-exclusive), and the fees being paid to the artist. It's also important to have a clear understanding of your rights as the artist and to make sure that the terms of the license agreement are clearly documented in writing.

By licensing your artwork, you can generate an additional stream of income and reach new audiences with your work. Just be sure to carefully consider the terms of any license agreement and make sure that you are being fairly compensated for the use of your artwork. In all cases, it's important to have a clear understanding of the terms of the license agreement and to make sure that you are being fairly compensated for the use of your artwork. It's also important to keep track of your earnings from licensed works and to report them as income on your taxes.

Teaching art classes and workshops is another way for artists to monetize their work. If you have a strong understanding of your art form and are able to effectively communicate your skills and knowledge to others, teaching art classes or workshops can be a great way to share your expertise and earn an income.

To teach art classes and workshops, you'll need to have a clear understanding of your subject matter and be able to effectively communicate your knowledge to others. You'll also need to have good organizational and time management skills to ensure that your classes run smoothly. You'll need to consider things like the content and structure of your classes, the materials and supplies that you'll need, and the length and frequency of your classes.

There are many different ways to teach art classes and workshops. You can teach in-person classes at a studio or community center, or you can teach online classes through platforms like Zoom or Google Meet. You can also teach one-time workshops or ongoing classes.
To market your art classes and workshops, you'll need to have a clear understanding of your target audience and how to reach them. You can use social media, email marketing, and in-person events like open studios or artist talks to promote your classes and build a following.
Here are some things you should consider when teaching art classes and workshops:

1. Preparing for your classes: To teach art classes or workshops, you'll need to have a clear understanding of your subject matter and be able to effectively communicate your knowledge to others. This may involve developing lesson plans, creating handouts or

other materials, and sourcing the necessary materials and supplies. You'll also need to consider things like the length and frequency of your classes, the size of your class, and the location of your classes.

2. Delivering your classes: When teaching art classes or workshops, it's important to be clear and organized in your delivery. This may involve demonstrating techniques, providing feedback and guidance to students, and answering questions. You'll also need to be flexible and able to adapt to the needs and skill levels of your students.

3. Marketing your classes: To attract students to your classes, you'll need to have a clear understanding of your target audience and how to reach them. You can use social media, email marketing, and in-person events like open studios or artist talks to promote your classes and build a following. You'll also need to consider things like pricing, payment methods, and cancellation policies.

4. Staying organized and managing your finances: Finally, it's important to stay organized and manage your finances as you teach art classes and workshops. This may involve keeping track of your income and expenses, setting goals, and budgeting for future classes. You'll also need to consider things like taxes and insurance, and make sure that you are properly compensated for your time and efforts.

Collaborating with other artists is another way for artists to monetize their work and build their careers. The power of collaboration lies in the ability to combine the skills, knowledge, and resources of multiple individuals to achieve a common goal. When artists collaborate, they can leverage the strengths of their partners to create something greater than they could achieve on their own.

There are many different ways that artists can collaborate, including:

1. Joint projects: Artists can collaborate on joint projects, such as exhibitions, installations, or public artworks. By working together, artists can pool their resources and leverage their collective talents to create something that is greater than the sum of its parts. When collaborating on joint projects, it's important to have a clear understanding of the goals and objectives of the project, as well as the roles and responsibilities of each collaborator. You'll need to communicate regularly with your collaborators and establish clear lines of communication to ensure that the project stays on track. You'll also need to consider things like deadlines, budgets, and the distribution of any profits or income from the project.

2. Cross-promotion: Artists can also collaborate by cross-promoting each other's work. This can involve sharing each other's work on social media, introducing each other to potential buyers or clients, or participating in joint exhibitions or events. When cross-promoting each other's work, it's important to be authentic and genuine in your support for your collaborators. You can share their work on social media, introduce them to potential buyers or clients, or participate in joint exhibitions or events together. By working together, you can build a stronger following and reach a wider audience with your work.

3. Resource sharing: Artists can also collaborate by sharing resources such as studios, tools, or equipment. This can be especially helpful for artists who are working

on a tight budget or who don't have access to certain resources. When sharing resources with other artists, it's important to establish clear rules and guidelines for their use. This may include things like scheduling, maintenance, and repair responsibilities, as well as any fees or charges that may be involved. It's also important to be considerate of your collaborators and respect their time and space when using shared resources.

4. Mentorship: Finally, artists can collaborate by mentoring each other or working together as apprentices. This can be an effective way for artists to share their skills and knowledge with others and help them develop their careers. When collaborating as mentors or apprentices, it's important to establish clear expectations and goals for the relationship. This may include things like the length of the mentorship, the frequency of meetings or sessions, and the specific areas of focus for the mentorship. It's also important to be open and honest with your mentee and provide constructive feedback to help them develop their skills and knowledge.

By collaborating with other artists, you can tap into the collective power of your network to achieve your goals and build your career. Just be sure to communicate clearly with your collaborators and establish clear roles and expectations to ensure a successful collaboration.

Diversifying your income streams is an important strategy for building a successful and sustainable career as an artist.

When you rely on a single source of income, you are vulnerable to changes in market conditions or other factors that could impact your income. By diversifying your income streams, you can reduce your risk and increase your financial stability. By diversifying your income streams, you can reduce your financial risk and build a more sustainable and rewarding career as an artist. Just be sure to carefully consider the opportunities that you pursue and make sure that they align with your goals and values as an artist.

CHAPTER 2

Developing a Strong Personal Brand

In the world of art, having a strong personal brand is essential for building a successful and sustainable career. In this chapter of 'The Art of Wealth: A Guide to Making Money as an Artist,' we explore the importance of developing a unique selling proposition, building a strong online presence, networking and building relationships, developing your skills and knowledge, and being consistent in your brand message and appearance.

This chapter will also cover how to establish your personal brand and how to use it to differentiate yourself from other artists in the market. You'll also learn about the benefits of developing a strong personal brand, such as the ability to attract more buyers and the chance to build a loyal customer base. By the end of this chapter, you'll have the tools and strategies you need to develop a strong personal brand effectively, and to achieve financial success as an artist. By following these tips, you can establish credibility, build trust with your audience, and set yourself apart from the competition as you grow your career as an artist.

Your personal brand is the unique combination of your skills, experience, personality, and values that sets you apart from other artists. It's what makes you memorable and distinguishes you from the competition. Here are a few tips for developing a strong personal brand as an artist:

1. Define your unique selling proposition (USP): Your USP is what makes you unique as an artist. It's what sets you apart from the competition and makes you memorable. To define your USP, ask yourself what you do differently than other artists, what makes your work unique, and what value you offer to your audience.
2. Build a strong online presence: In today's digital world, having a strong online presence is essential for artists. This includes having a website or portfolio, as well as an active presence on social media. Use these platforms to showcase your work, share your thoughts and ideas, and engage with your audience.
3. Network and build relationships: Building relationships with other artists, gallerists, collectors, and other industry professionals can help you build your personal brand and grow your career. Attend events, join artist groups and associations, and reach out to others to build your network.
4. Develop your skills and knowledge: To build a strong personal brand as an artist, it's important to continually develop your skills and knowledge. This may involve taking classes, workshops, or online courses, as well as experimenting with new techniques and media.
5. Be consistent: Finally, it's important to be consistent in your brand message and appearance. This includes everything from the way you present yourself online to the way you interact with others. By being consistent, you can establish credibility and build trust with your audience.

By developing a strong personal brand, you can differentiate yourself from other artists and build a more rewarding and successful career.

Defining your brand as an artist is an important first step in developing a strong personal brand. Your brand is the unique combination of your skills, experience, personality, and values that sets you apart from other artists. It's the way that people perceive you and your work, and it influences the opportunities that you attract and the value that people place on your work.
Here are a few steps to help you define your brand as an artist:

1. Identify your unique skills and talents: What sets you apart as an artist? What skills and talents do you bring to your work? Consider your unique perspective, style, or approach to your art form.
2. Define your values and beliefs: What values and beliefs do you hold dear as an artist? What do you stand for, and what is important to you as an artist? Consider your motivations and the message that you want to convey through your work.
3. Determine your target audience: Who is your target audience as an artist? Who do you want to reach with your work, and what do they value in an artist? Consider the demographics, interests, and values of your ideal audience.
4. Develop your brand positioning: Based on your unique skills and talents, values and beliefs, and target audience, develop a clear and compelling positioning for your brand. This should be a short, clear statement that summarizes who you are as an artist and what you stand for.

By defining your brand as an artist, you can create a clear and consistent message that resonates with your audience and sets you apart from other artists. This will help you attract the right opportunities and build a more rewarding and successful career.

Building a strong online presence is essential for artists in today's digital age. Your online presence is the way that people perceive you and your work online, and it can influence the opportunities that you attract and the value that people place on your work.
Here are a few tips for building a strong online presence as an artist:

1. Create a website: Having a website is an essential part of building a strong online presence as an artist. Your website should showcase your work and tell your story, and it should be easy to navigate and use. Be sure to include high-quality images of your work, as well as information about your background, experience, and the message that you want to convey through your work. Your website is the central hub of your online presence and should be the first place that people go to learn about you and your work. In addition to showcasing your work, your website should also include information about your background, experience, and the message that you want to convey through your work. You should also include contact information and links to your social media profiles to make it easy for people to get in touch with you.
2. Use social media: Social media platforms like Instagram, Facebook, and Twitter are powerful tools for building a strong online presence as an artist. Use these platforms to share your work, connect with your audience, and build a following. Be sure to post regularly and engage with your followers to build a strong and active community. Social media platforms like Instagram, Facebook, and Twitter are powerful tools for building a

strong online presence as an artist. Use these platforms to share your work, connect with your audience, and build a following. Be sure to post regularly and engage with your followers to build a strong and active community. You should also use hashtags and tag other artists and galleries in your posts to increase your visibility and reach.

3. Engage with your audience: Building a strong online presence is about more than just sharing your work. It's also about engaging with your audience and building relationships with them. Respond to comments and messages, ask for feedback, and share behind-the-scenes glimpses of your process to build a deeper connection with your audience. Building a strong online presence is about more than just sharing your work. It's also about engaging with your audience and building relationships with them. Respond to comments and messages, ask for feedback, and share behind-the-scenes glimpses of your process to build a deeper connection with your audience. You should also consider hosting live streams or Q&A sessions to give your audience a chance to interact with you in real-time.

4. Use SEO: Search engine optimization (SEO) is the practice of optimizing your website and online content to rank higher in search engine results. By using SEO strategies like keyword research and on-page optimization, you can improve the visibility of your website and reach more people with your work. Search engine optimization (SEO) is the practice of optimizing your website and online content to rank higher in search engine results. By using SEO strategies like keyword research and on-page optimization, you can improve the visibility of your website and reach more people with your work. You should also consider using tools

like Google Analytics to track the performance of your website and identify opportunities for improvement.

By building a strong online presence, you can reach a wider audience with your work and build a more rewarding and successful career as an artist.

* * *

Networking and building relationships is an important part of building a successful career as an artist. Building relationships with other artists, galleries, collectors, and industry professionals can be a powerful way to build your personal brand and attract new opportunities.
Here are a few tips for networking and building relationships as an artist:

1. Attend events and exhibitions: Attending events and exhibitions is a great way to meet other artists, galleries, collectors, and industry professionals. You can network with these individuals and build relationships by introducing yourself, sharing your work, and engaging in conversations about your art form.
2. Join artist groups and associations: Joining artist groups and associations is another way to build relationships with other artists. These groups often host events, workshops, and exhibitions that provide opportunities for artists to connect and collaborate. You can also participate in online forums and communities to connect with other artists and share your work and ideas.
3. Reach out to others in your field: You can also build relationships by reaching out to other artists, galleries, collectors, and industry professionals directly. This can involve sending emails, making phone calls, or

connecting with people on social media. Just be sure to be genuine and respectful in your communications and be prepared to follow up and nurture these relationships over time.
4. Collaborate with others: Collaborating with other artists is another way to build relationships and strengthen your network. You can collaborate on joint projects, cross-promote each other's work, share resources, or work together as mentors or apprentices. By collaborating with others, you can tap into the collective power of your network to achieve your goals and build your career.

By networking and building relationships, you can build a stronger network of contacts and open up new opportunities for your career as an artist. Just be sure to be authentic, genuine, and respectful in your interactions with others, and be prepared to follow up and nurture these relationships over time.

Developing your skills and knowledge is an important part of building a strong personal brand as an artist. By continually learning and improving your skills, you can stay competitive and relevant in the art world and build a more sustainable and rewarding career.

Here are a few ways that artists can develop their skills and knowledge:

1. Take classes or workshops: One way to develop your skills and knowledge is by taking classes or workshops. These can be in-person or online and can cover a wide range of subjects, from techniques and materials to business and marketing.
2. Experiment with new techniques and media: Another way to develop your skills is by experimenting with new techniques and media. This can involve trying out new

materials or techniques in your work, or incorporating new styles or approaches into your art.
3. Read and research: Reading and researching can also help you develop your skills and knowledge as an artist. This can include reading books, articles, or blog posts about your art form, as well as staying up-to-date on industry trends and developments.
4. Join artist groups and associations: Joining artist groups and associations can also help you develop your skills and knowledge. These organizations often offer workshops, classes, and other educational opportunities, as well as networking and mentorship opportunities.
5. Seek out mentors or apprenticeships: Finally, seeking out mentors or apprenticeships can be a great way to develop your skills and knowledge as an artist. Working with a mentor or participating in an apprenticeship can provide you with valuable guidance, feedback, and support as you develop your career.

CHAPTER 3

Finding Your Niche and Target Market

Finding your niche and target market is essential for building a successful and sustainable career as an artist. In this chapter of 'The Art of Wealth: A Guide to Making Money as an Artist,' we explore how to identify your unique selling proposition, research your target market, and position your art for success.

By following these strategies, you can tap into your strengths and passions as an artist and build a career that is both fulfilling and financially rewarding. This chapter will also cover how to develop a clear and consistent brand message and how to use market research to better understand your target audience. You'll also learn about the benefits of finding your niche and target market, such as the ability to stand out in a crowded market and the chance to build a loyal customer base. By the end of this chapter, you'll have the tools and strategies you need to find your niche and target market effectively, and to achieve financial success as an artist.

Your niche is the specific area or focus of your art, while your target market is the group of people who are most likely to be interested in your art. By identifying your niche and target market, you can better understand your unique strengths and passions as an artist and position your art for success.

Here are a few steps for finding your niche and target market as an artist:

Identify your unique selling proposition (USP): Your USP is what sets you apart from other artists and makes you memorable. To identify your USP, ask yourself what you do differently than other artists, what makes your work unique, and what value you offer to your audience. Your USP should be based on your unique skills, experience, and perspective as an artist, and should reflect your values and goals as a creative professional. Identifying your unique selling proposition (USP) is an essential step for building a successful and sustainable career as an artist. Your USP is what sets you apart from other artists and makes you memorable. It's the unique combination of your skills, experience, personality, and values that makes your art stand out and adds value to your audience.

Reflect on your strengths and passions: To identify your USP, it's important to first reflect on your strengths and passions as an artist. What are your unique skills and techniques? What subjects or themes do you enjoy exploring in your art? What value do you bring to your work? By understanding your strengths and passions, you can begin to identify the elements of your art that make you unique.

Consider your target market: Another important factor to consider when identifying your USP is your target market. Who are the people who are most likely to be interested in your art? What are their interests and preferences? What are their needs and expectations? By understanding your target market, you can better tailor your USP to their needs and preferences.

Research your target market: Once you've identified your USP, the next step is to research your target market. This involves understanding the demographics, interests, and needs of the people who are most likely to be interested in your art. You can research your target market by conducting surveys, analyzing industry data, and talking to potential buyers or collectors. Some key questions to consider when researching your target market include: Who are they? What are their interests and preferences? What motivates them to buy art? What are their budget constraints? What are their expectations for quality and value? By answering these questions, you can gain a better understanding of your target market and tailor your art and marketing efforts to meet their needs and preferences. Researching your target market is an essential step for building a successful and sustainable career as an artist. Your target market is the group of people who are most likely to be interested in your art. By understanding the demographics, interests, and needs of your target market, you can tailor your pricing, marketing, and online presence to better resonate with them.

Conduct market research: Market research is the process of gathering and analyzing data about your target market. This can involve conducting surveys, focus groups, or interviews with potential buyers or collectors, as well as analyzing industry data and trends. By conducting market research, you can gain valuable insights into your target market and better understand their needs and preferences.

Analyze your competition: Another way to identify your USP is to analyze your competition. What are other artists in your field doing differently? What value do they offer to their audience? How can you differentiate your art from theirs? By understanding your competition, you can identify opportunities to set yourself apart and offer something unique to your audience.

Test and refine your USP: It's important to test and refine your USP to ensure that it resonates with your audience. This may involve gathering feedback from potential buyers or collectors, experimenting with different marketing approaches, or adjusting your pricing or online presence. By testing and refining your USP, you can ensure that it accurately reflects the value and uniqueness of your art.

Use online tools and resources: There are many online tools and resources that can help you research your target market. These can include social media analytics, website analytics, and online marketplaces that provide data on the preferences and behaviors of their users. By using these tools and resources, you can gather valuable data on your target market and use it to inform your marketing and sales efforts.

Network and build relationships: Networking and building relationships can also be valuable sources of information about your target market. By interacting with potential buyers, collectors, and other industry professionals, you can gain insights into their needs and preferences and use this information to better position your art for success.

Position your art for success: Once you have a clear understanding of your niche and target market, you can position your art for success. This may involve adjusting your pricing, marketing strategies, or online presence to better align with your target market. It may also involve seeking out opportunities to showcase your work, such as exhibitions, events, or online platforms. When positioning your art for success, it's important to be proactive and take a strategic approach. This may involve identifying and targeting specific markets or demographics, developing targeted marketing campaigns, or building relationships with key influencers or decision-makers in the art world.

* * *

Positioning your art for success is an essential step for building a successful and sustainable career as an artist. This involves understanding your unique selling proposition, researching your target market, and adapting your pricing, marketing, and online presence to better align with your target audience.

By positioning your art for success, you can tap into your strengths and passions as an artist and build a career that is both fulfilling and financially rewarding. To position your art for success, it's important to understand your USP and use it to your advantage. This may involve focusing on specific techniques, styles, or mediums that differentiate your art from the competition, or highlighting the unique value or perspective that you bring to your work.

Knowing your target market is an important part of positioning your art for success. By understanding the demographics, interests, and needs of the people who are most likely to be interested in your art, you can tailor your pricing, marketing, and online presence to better resonate with them.

Adjust your pricing strategy: Pricing your art effectively is an important aspect of positioning your art for success. There are several different approaches to pricing your art, including cost-based pricing, value-based pricing, and competition-based pricing. By understanding your costs and expenses and considering your target market, you can develop a pricing strategy that works for you.

Develop a strong online presence: In today's digital age, having a strong online presence is essential for artists. This includes having a website or portfolio, as well as an active presence on social media. Use these platforms to showcase your work, share your thoughts and ideas, and engage with your audience.

Seek out opportunities to showcase your work: Finally, positioning your art for success may involve seeking out opportunities to showcase your work, such as exhibitions, events, or online platforms. By showcasing your art in different contexts, you can reach new audiences and build your reputation as an artist.

Develop a clear and consistent brand message: Developing a clear and consistent brand message is an important part of building a successful career as an artist. Your brand message is the unique combination of your skills, experience, personality, and values that sets you apart from other artists. It's what makes you memorable and distinguishes you from the competition.

Define your brand's core values: Your brand's core values are the guiding principles that inform your art and your approach to your career. These values should reflect your goals and priorities as an artist and should be reflected in your work and your interactions with others.

Develop a consistent visual identity: A consistent visual identity is an important part of developing a clear and consistent brand message. This includes everything from your logo and color scheme to your website design and social media presence. By creating a cohesive and consistent visual identity, you can establish credibility and build trust with your audience.

Communicate clearly and consistently: Finally, it's important to communicate clearly and consistently in order to develop a clear and consistent brand message. This includes everything from the way you present yourself online to the way you interact with others. By being consistent in your brand message and appearance, you can establish credibility and build trust with your audience.

You should now be able to find your niche and target market to build your successful and sustainable career as an artist. We have explored how to identify your unique selling proposition, research your target market, and position your art for success. With these strategies, you can now build a career that is both fulfilling and financially rewarding.

CHAPTER 4

Pricing Your Artwork Effectively

In 'Pricing Your Artwork Effectively,' learn the strategies and techniques for setting competitive prices for your art that will help you maximize your income and achieve financial success. Discover how to consider your costs and expenses, research your target market, and use pricing strategies to set the right price for your art.

This chapter will provide you with the knowledge and skills you need to price your artwork effectively and achieve financial success as an artist. This chapter will also cover how to test and adjust your pricing to ensure that you are maximizing your income and how to communicate your prices to potential buyers. You'll also learn about the importance of pricing your artwork effectively, such as the ability to attract more buyers and the chance to achieve financial success as an artist. By the end of this chapter, you'll have the tools and strategies you need to price your artwork effectively, and to achieve financial success as an artist.

Pricing your artwork effectively is an important aspect of building a successful and sustainable career as an artist. Properly pricing your art can help you attract the right buyers, build your reputation, and generate income. However, pricing your art can be challenging, as it involves balancing the value of your work with the needs and expectations of your target market.

There is a generally accepted formula for pricing paintings that involves multiplying the dimensions of the artwork (height plus width) by an artist's "index number." This "index number" can vary depending on the artist's experience and level of recognition in the art world. For beginners, an index number between 5 and 10 is appropriate. For more experienced painters who are taking their work seriously, an index between 10 and 15 is recommended.

As an artist begins to exhibit their work in galleries and establish a reputation, an index between 15 and 25 may be appropriate. It is important to note that this is just a general guideline and ultimately the price of a painting will depend on various factors such as the materials used, the size and complexity of the work, and the artist's personal pricing strategy. While the formula is generally accepted there are still some key aspects you as an artist should take into consideration.

Consider your costs and expenses: The first step in pricing your artwork is to understand your costs and expenses. This includes everything from the cost of materials and studio rent to marketing and promotional expenses. By understanding your costs, you can ensure that your pricing covers these expenses and allows you to make a profit. Considering your costs and expenses is an important step in pricing your artwork effectively. Your costs and expenses are the various expenses that you incur in the process of creating and selling your art. These may include the cost of materials, studio rent, marketing and promotional expenses, and any other costs associated with your art career.

Here are a few tips for considering your costs and expenses when pricing your artwork:

1. Keep track of your costs: The first step in considering your costs and expenses is to keep track of them. This may involve keeping receipts for materials and supplies, tracking your studio rent and other expenses, and maintaining a budget for your art career. By keeping track of your costs, you can get a clear picture of the expenses associated with your art and use this information to inform your pricing decisions.

2. Determine your profit margin: Once you have a clear understanding of your costs and expenses, the next step is to determine your profit margin. Your profit margin is the difference between your costs and the price at which you sell your art. For example, if you sell a painting for $100 and your costs are $50, your profit margin is $50. By determining your profit margin, you can ensure that you are pricing your art effectively and making a profit.

3. Adjust your pricing based on your costs: Finally, it's important to adjust your pricing based on your costs and expenses. This may involve adjusting your pricing up or down based on changes in your costs, or using different pricing strategies to cover your costs and achieve your desired profit margin. By considering your costs and expenses when pricing your art, you can ensure that you are pricing your artwork effectively and making a profit.

Research your target market: Knowing your target market is

also important when it comes to pricing your artwork. By understanding the demographics, interests, and needs of the people who are most likely to be interested in your art, you can tailor your pricing to better resonate with them. Your target market is the group of people who are most likely to be interested in your art. By understanding the demographics, interests, and needs of your target market, you can tailor your pricing, marketing, and online presence to better resonate with them.

Here are a few tips for researching your target market:

1. Identify your unique selling proposition (USP): Your USP is what sets you apart from other artists and makes you memorable. To research your target market, it's important to first identify your USP and understand the value that you offer to your audience.

2. Conduct market research: Market research is the process of gathering and analyzing data about your target market. This can involve conducting surveys, focus groups, or interviews with potential buyers or collectors, as well as analyzing industry data and trends. By conducting market research, you can gain valuable insights into your target market and better understand their needs and preferences.

3. Use online tools and resources: There are many online tools and resources that can help you research your target market. These can include social media analytics, website analytics, and online marketplaces that provide data on the preferences and behaviors of their users. By using these tools and resources, you can gather valuable data on your target market and use it to inform your marketing and sales efforts.

4. Network and build relationships: Networking and building relationships can also be valuable sources of information about your target market. By interacting with potential buyers, collectors, and other industry professionals, you can gain insights into their needs and preferences and use this information to better position your art for success.

Use pricing strategies: There are several different pricing strategies that you can use when pricing your artwork. These include cost-based pricing, value-based pricing, and competition-based pricing. Cost-based pricing involves setting your price based on the cost of materials and production, while value-based pricing involves setting your price based on the perceived value of your art to the buyer.

Competition-based pricing involves setting your price based on the prices of other artists in your field. By using a pricing strategy that makes sense for your art and your target market, you can ensure that you are pricing your artwork effectively. There are several different pricing strategies that you can use when pricing your artwork. These strategies can help you balance the value of your work with the needs and expectations of your target market, and ensure that you are pricing your art effectively.

Here are a few common pricing strategies that you can use when pricing your artwork:

1. Cost-based pricing: Cost-based pricing involves setting your price based on the cost of materials and production. This approach works well if you have a

clear understanding of your costs and expenses and want to ensure that your pricing covers these expenses and allows you to make a profit. To use this pricing strategy, you will need to have a clear understanding of your costs and expenses, including the cost of materials, studio rent, marketing and promotional expenses, and any other costs associated with your art career. Once you have a clear understanding of your costs, you can set your price based on the amount you need to cover these expenses and make a profit.

2. Value-based pricing: Value-based pricing involves setting your price based on the perceived value of your art to the buyer. This approach works well if you have a unique or highly sought-after product and want to price it based on its value to the buyer. Value-based pricing involves setting your price based on the perceived value of your art to the buyer. To use this pricing strategy, you will need to understand the value that your art offers to your audience and set your price accordingly. This may involve considering the uniqueness, quality, or rarity of your art, as well as any other factors that add value to your audience.

3. Competition-based pricing: Competition-based pricing involves setting your price based on the prices of other artists in your field. This approach works well if you want to be competitive with other artists in your market and ensure that your pricing is in line with industry standards. Competition-based pricing involves setting your price based on the prices of other artists in your field. To use this pricing strategy, you will need to research the prices of similar artists in your market and ensure that your pricing is competitive. This approach can help you stay competitive in your market and ensure that your pricing is in line with industry standards.

4. Premium pricing: Premium pricing involves setting a high price for your art based on the perceived value and exclusivity of your product. This approach works well if you have a unique or high-quality product that commands a higher price due to its rarity or perceived value. Premium pricing involves setting a high price for your art based on the perceived value and exclusivity of your product. To use this pricing strategy, you will need to have a unique or high-quality product that commands a higher price due to its rarity or perceived value. This approach can be effective if you have a highly sought-after product that is perceived as being of higher value than similar products in the market.

Test and adjust your pricing: Finally, it's important to test and adjust your pricing to ensure that it is effective. This may involve gathering feedback from buyers or collectors, experimenting with different pricing strategies, or adjusting your pricing based on market trends or changes in your costs.

By testing and adjusting your pricing, you can ensure that it accurately reflects the value of your art and meets the needs and expectations of your target market. Testing and adjusting your pricing is an important step in ensuring that you are pricing your artwork effectively. Testing and adjusting your pricing involves gathering feedback from buyers or collectors, experimenting with different pricing strategies, and adjusting your pricing based on market trends or changes in your costs.

Here are a few tips for testing and adjusting your pricing:

1. Gather feedback from buyers or collectors: One way

to test and adjust your pricing is to gather feedback from buyers or collectors. This may involve asking for feedback on your pricing through surveys, focus groups, or one-on-one conversations. By gathering feedback from buyers or collectors, you can gain valuable insights into their perceptions of the value of your art and use this information to adjust your pricing.

2. Experiment with different pricing strategies: Another way to test and adjust your pricing is to experiment with different pricing strategies. This may involve using different pricing structures, such as tiered pricing or bundle pricing, or experimenting with different price points to see how they impact sales. By experimenting with different pricing strategies, you can gain a better understanding of what works and what doesn't and adjust your pricing accordingly.

3. Adjust your pricing based on market trends or changes in your costs: Finally, it's important to adjust your pricing based on market trends or changes in your costs. This may involve adjusting your pricing up or down based on changes in demand or the prices of similar products in the market, or adjusting your pricing based on changes in your costs, such as the cost of materials or studio rent. By regularly reviewing and adjusting your pricing, you can ensure that it accurately reflects the value of your art and meets the needs and expectations of your target market.

Finally, when working with galleries to sell your original artwork, typically the artist does not have to pay a commission or fee for the gallery's representation or promotion of their work. The artist and gallery agree on a retail price for each artwork, which is listed in a written price list. The artist retains ownership of the artwork until it is sold.

The gallery earns money by selling the artist's artwork and profits are split 50-50% between the artist and the gallery. The gallery may offer a discount on the artwork to certain clients with the artist's permission, and in the case of a museum acquiring the artwork, the discount may be up to 50% due to the benefits it brings to the artist's resume. It is not allowed for the artist to sell an artwork that is consigned to the gallery for a specific exhibition.

CHAPTER 5

Selling Your Art Online

In 'Selling Your Art Online,' you will learn the strategies and techniques for effectively selling your art online, and reach a wider audience. Discover how to choose the right platform, create a professional online presence, use high-quality images, set competitive prices, and promote your art.

This chapter will provide you with the knowledge and skills you need to sell your art online and achieve financial success as an artist. This chapter will also cover how to create a professional online portfolio and how to use online tools and platforms to showcase and sell your art. You'll also learn about the benefits of selling your art online, such as the ability to reach a global audience and the convenience of being able to sell your art from anywhere. By the end of this chapter, you'll have the tools and strategies you need to sell your art online effectively, and to achieve financial success as an artist.

Selling your art online is a great way to reach a wider audience and generate income as an artist. The internet provides a vast, global platform for artists to showcase and sell their work, and there are many online marketplaces and platforms that can help artists get started.

✱ ✱ ✱

Choose the right platform:

There are many online platforms and marketplaces available for artists to sell their work, including websites, social media, and online marketplaces like Etsy and eBay. It's important to choose a platform that aligns with your goals and target market and provides the features and tools that you need to succeed. Choosing the right platform for selling your art online is an important step in building a successful and sustainable career as an artist. There are many different online platforms and marketplaces available, each with its own unique features and benefits.

Here are a few things to consider when choosing the right platform for your art:

1. Your goals: The first thing to consider when choosing a platform is your goals. What do you hope to achieve by selling your art online? Do you want to reach a wider audience, generate income, or both? Understanding your goals will help you choose a platform that aligns with your needs and expectations.

2. Your target market: It's also important to consider your target market when choosing a platform. Different platforms attract different types of buyers, so it's important to choose a platform that aligns with the demographics, interests, and needs of your target market.

3. The platform's features and tools: Each platform has

its own set of features and tools, so it's important to choose a platform that provides the features and tools you need to succeed. This may include things like payment processing, shipping options, marketing tools, and customer support.

4. The platform's fees and policies: Finally, it's important to consider the fees and policies of the platform you choose. Some platforms charge fees for listing or selling your art, while others may have restrictions on the types of art you can sell or the way you sell it. It's important to understand the fees and policies of the platform you choose and ensure that they align with your goals and expectations.

* * *

Create a professional online presence:

To sell your art online, you will need to create a professional online presence. This may involve building a website or creating a social media profile, as well as establishing a brand and creating a cohesive, visually appealing portfolio of your work. Creating a professional online presence is an important step in building a successful and sustainable career as an artist. Your online presence is often the first thing that potential buyers or collectors see, and it's important to make a good first impression.

Here are a few tips for creating a professional online presence:

1. Build a website: Building a website is a great way to showcase your art and create a professional online

presence. Your website should include a portfolio of your work, as well as information about your background, style, and process. You can use a website builder like Wix or Squarespace to create a professional-looking website quickly and easily.

2. Use social media: Social media is another great way to create a professional online presence and reach a wider audience. Choose the social media platforms that align with your goals and target market and use them to showcase your art and engage with potential buyers or collectors.

3. Establish a brand: Establishing a brand is an important part of creating a professional online presence. Your brand is the visual and emotional image that people associate with your art, and it helps to differentiate you from other artists. Consider your brand elements, such as your logo, color scheme, and typography, and use them consistently across your online presence.

4. Create a cohesive, visually appealing portfolio: Finally, it's important to create a cohesive, visually appealing portfolio of your work. Use high-quality, visually appealing images of your art and organize them in a way that makes sense and showcases your style and process. Your portfolio should be easy to navigate and give potential buyers a clear sense of what you offer.

* * *

Use high-quality images:

The images of your art that you use online will be the first thing that potential buyers see, so it's important to use high-quality, visually appealing images that accurately represent your work. Use a good camera or smartphone and take multiple shots of your work from different angles to give buyers a clear sense of what they are purchasing. Using high-quality images is an important aspect of selling your art online. The images of your art that you use online will be the first thing that potential buyers see, so it's important to use high-quality, visually appealing images that accurately represent your work.

Here are a few tips for using high-quality images when selling your art online:

1. Use a good camera or smartphone: To get the best images of your art, it's important to use a good camera or smartphone. Look for a device with a high-resolution camera and good low-light performance to ensure that your images are clear and detailed.

2. Take multiple shots: It's a good idea to take multiple shots of your art from different angles to give buyers a clear sense of what they are purchasing. This may include close-ups of details, as well as wider shots that show the entire piece.

3. Edit and retouch your images: Editing and retouching your images can help to enhance their quality and make them more visually appealing. There are many photo editing tools available that can help you improve the lighting, color, and composition of your images.

4. Use image formats and sizes appropriately: Finally, it's important to use image formats and sizes appropriately when selling your art online. Different platforms have different requirements for image formats and sizes, so it's important to follow their guidelines to ensure that

your images look their best.

By using high-quality images, you can showcase your art in the best possible light and attract more buyers and collectors online.

* * *

Set competitive prices:

When selling your art online, it's important to set competitive prices that reflect the value of your work and align with the needs and expectations of your target market. Research similar artists and the prices they are charging, and use pricing strategies like cost-based pricing, value-based pricing, or competition-based pricing to set your prices. Setting competitive prices is an important aspect of selling your art online. By setting competitive prices, you can attract the right buyers, build your reputation, and generate income as an artist. However, pricing your art can be challenging, as it involves balancing the value of your work with the needs and expectations of your target market.

Here are a few tips for setting competitive prices for your art online:

1. Research similar artists and the prices they are charging: One way to set competitive prices is to research similar artists and the prices they are charging. This can give you a sense of the market rate for art in your medium and help you ensure that your prices are competitive.

2. Use pricing strategies: There are several different pricing

strategies that you can use when pricing your art online. These include cost-based pricing, value-based pricing, and competition-based pricing. Cost-based pricing involves setting your price based on the cost of materials and production, while value-based pricing involves setting your price based on the perceived value of your art to the buyer. Competition-based pricing involves setting your price based on the prices of other artists in your field. By using a pricing strategy that makes sense for your art and your target market, you can set competitive prices.

3. Consider your costs and expenses: It's also important to consider your costs and expenses when setting your prices. This includes things like the cost of materials, studio rent, and marketing and promotional expenses. By understanding your costs, you can ensure that your pricing covers these expenses and allows you to make a profit.

4. Test and adjust your pricing: Finally, it's important to test and adjust your pricing to ensure that it is effective. This may involve gathering feedback from buyers or collectors, experimenting with different pricing strategies, or adjusting your pricing based on market trends or changes in your costs. By testing and adjusting your pricing, you can ensure that it accurately reflects the value of your art and meets the needs and expectations of your target market.

❊ ❊ ❊

Promote your art:

Finally, it's important to promote your art and get the word out about your work. This may involve using social media, email marketing, or other marketing techniques to reach your target audience and showcase your art to potential buyers. Promoting your art is an important step in building a successful and sustainable career as an artist. By promoting your art, you can reach a wider audience, generate income, and build your reputation. There are many different ways to promote your art online, and the best approach will depend on your goals, target market, and resources.

Here are a few tips for promoting your art online:

1. Use social media: Social media is a great way to promote your art and reach a wider audience. Choose the social media platforms that align with your goals and target market and use them to showcase your art and engage with potential buyers or collectors.

2. Use email marketing: Email marketing is another effective way to promote your art. By building an email list and sending newsletters or promotional emails to your subscribers, you can keep them informed about your new art, exhibitions, and other updates.

3. Participate in online art communities: Participating in online art communities and forums can help you connect with other artists and collectors and promote your art. Look for art-specific communities and forums or join broader communities that align with your interests and target market.

4. Use paid advertising: Finally, you can use paid advertising to promote your art online. There are many different paid advertising options available, including Google Ads, social media ads, and display ads. Paid

advertising can be an effective way to reach a targeted audience and generate leads, but it's important to set a budget and track your results to ensure that you are getting a good return on your investment.

CHAPTER 6

Marketing Your Art and Building a Following

In 'Marketing Your Art and Building a Following,' learn the strategies and techniques for effectively marketing your art and building a following of loyal fans and customers. Discover how to create a strong online presence, use social media and online platforms, create a marketing plan, and engage with your audience.

This chapter will also cover how to create high-quality images of your art and how to use them effectively in your marketing efforts, as well as how to create a strong and consistent brand message. You'll also learn about the benefits of marketing your art and building a following, such as the ability to reach a wider audience and the chance to build a loyal customer base. By the end of this chapter, you'll have the tools and strategies you need to market your art and build a following effectively, and to achieve financial success as an artist.

Marketing your art and building a following is an important step in building a successful and sustainable career as an artist. By marketing your art and building a following, you can reach a wider audience, generate income, and build your reputation. Here are a few tips for marketing your art and building a following online:

Create a strong online presence: Creating a strong online presence is an important aspect of marketing your art and building a following. This may involve building a website, creating a social media profile, or establishing a brand. Your online presence should showcase your art, provide information about your background and process, and engage with potential buyers or collectors.

Use social media effectively: Social media is a powerful tool for marketing your art and building a following. Choose the social media platforms that align with your goals and target market and use them to showcase your art, engage with your followers, and share updates and insights about your work.

Use email marketing: Email marketing is another effective way to market your art and build a following. By building an email list and sending newsletters or promotional emails to your subscribers, you can keep them informed about your new art, exhibitions, and other updates.

Participate in online art communities: Participating in online art communities and forums can help you connect with other artists and collectors and promote your art. Look for art-specific communities and forums or join broader communities that align with your interests and target market.

Here are a few additional tips that may be helpful:

Use paid advertising: You can also use paid advertising to market your art and build a following. There are many different paid advertising options available, including Google Ads, social media ads, and display ads. Paid advertising can be an effective way to reach a targeted audience and generate leads, but it's important to set a budget and track your results to ensure that you are getting a good return on your investment.

1. Create high-quality, shareable content: Creating high-quality, shareable content is a great way to market your art and build a following. This may include blog posts, videos, podcasts, or other forms of content that showcase your art and provide value to your audience. By creating content that is interesting, informative, or entertaining, you can attract more followers and establish yourself as a thought leader in your field.

2. Use SEO (search engine optimization): SEO is the practice of optimizing your online content and presence to rank higher in search engine results. By using relevant keywords and phrases in your website and social media content, you can improve your visibility and attract more traffic from search engines.

3. Collaborate with other artists: Collaborating with other artists is a great way to market your art and build a following. By working with other artists, you can reach a wider audience, cross-promote each other's work, and learn from each other. You can collaborate by exhibiting together, creating art together, or promoting each other's work online.

4. Utilize influencer marketing: Influencer marketing is the practice of partnering with influencers, who are people with a large and engaged following, to promote

your art. Influencer marketing can be an effective way to reach a wider audience and build credibility, but it's important to choose influencers who align with your brand and target market.

5. Host events or exhibitions: Hosting events or exhibitions is another way to market your art and build a following. By hosting exhibitions or events, you can showcase your art in person, meet potential buyers or collectors, and build your reputation as an artist.

CHAPTER 7

Getting Representation and Working with Galleries

In 'Getting Representation and Working with Galleries,' learn the strategies and techniques for effectively getting representation and working with galleries to showcase and sell your art. Discover how to build a relationship with the gallery, understand gallery contracts, follow gallery submission guidelines, show your work in a professional manner, network with other artists and gallerists, attend art fairs and exhibitions, and submit your portfolio.

This chapter will also cover how to create a professional portfolio and how to research galleries to find the best fit for your art. You'll also learn about the benefits of getting representation and working with galleries, such as the opportunity to showcase your art to a wider audience and the chance to build a relationship with a professional art dealer. By the end of this chapter, you'll have the tools and strategies you need to get representation and work with galleries effectively, and to achieve financial success as an artist.

Getting representation and working with galleries is an important step in building a successful and sustainable career as an artist.

Representation can help you reach a wider audience, build your reputation, and generate income.

* * *

Here are a few tips for getting representation and working with galleries:

Research galleries: One of the first steps in getting representation is to research galleries that align with your style and goals. Look for galleries that represent artists in your medium, genre, or style and that have a reputation for supporting and promoting artists. Here are a few tips for researching galleries:

1. Identify your target galleries: Identify galleries that align with your style and goals. Research the galleries' focus and mission, the types of artists they represent, and the types of art they show.

2. Research the gallery's reputation: Research the gallery's reputation and track record. Look for reviews, articles, or other information about the gallery and its exhibitions. This can give you a sense of the gallery's credibility and success.

3. Research the gallery's audience: Research the gallery's audience, including the types of buyers and collectors the gallery attracts, and the gallery's location and demographics. This can help you understand the potential market for your art.

4. Research the gallery's submission guidelines: Research the gallery's submission guidelines and follow them exactly. This may include guidelines for the materials you need to submit (e.g., images, resume, statement),

and the process for submitting your work.

Create a professional portfolio: To get representation, you'll need to create a professional portfolio of your art. Your portfolio should showcase your best work and give a sense of your style and process. Use high-quality images and present your work in a cohesive and visually appealing way. Here are a few tips for creating a professional portfolio:

1. Choose your best work: Choose your best work to include in your portfolio. This should be a selection of your most recent, high-quality, and representative art. Consider the focus and mission of the galleries you are targeting and choose work that aligns with their interests.

2. Use high-quality images: Use high-quality images of your art in your portfolio. These images should be clear, well-lit, and accurately represent your art.

3. Present your work in a cohesive and visually appealing way: Present your work in a cohesive and visually appealing way. This may involve grouping your art by theme, medium, or style, or using a consistent layout or design.

4. Include a resume or CV: Include a resume or CV in your portfolio that outlines your education, exhibitions, awards, and other relevant information.

5. Write an artist statement: Write an artist statement that provides context for your art and showcases your style and process. This statement should be concise, informative, and engaging, and should give the reader a sense of your artistic vision and goals.

By creating a professional portfolio, you can showcase your work and stand out from other artists, which can increase your chances of getting representation and working with galleries.

Submit your portfolio: Once you have a professional portfolio, you can start submitting it to galleries for consideration. Many galleries have specific submission guidelines, so be sure to follow these carefully. You may need to submit images of your work, a resume, and a statement about your art and goals. Here are a few tips for submitting your portfolio:

1. Choose your best work: Choose your best work to include in your portfolio. This should be a selection of your most recent, high-quality, and representative art. Consider the focus and mission of the gallery you are submitting to and choose work that aligns with their interests.

2. Use high-quality images: Use high-quality images of your art in your portfolio. These images should be clear, well-lit, and accurately represent your art.

3. Include a resume: Include a resume or CV in your portfolio that outlines your education, exhibitions, awards, and other relevant information.

4. Write an artist statement: Write an artist statement that provides context for your art and showcases your style and process. This statement should be concise, informative, and engaging, and should give the reader a sense of your artistic vision and goals.

Attend art fairs and exhibitions: Attending art fairs and exhibitions is another way to get representation and build relationships with galleries. Art fairs and exhibitions are great places to meet galleries and other artists and showcase your work. Here are a few tips for attending art fairs and exhibitions:

1. Research and apply to art fairs and exhibitions: Research art fairs and exhibitions that align with your style and goals, and apply to participate. Many art fairs and exhibitions have specific submission guidelines and deadlines, so be sure to follow these carefully.

2. Prepare your art: Prepare your art for display at the art fair or exhibition. This may involve framing your art, creating display materials (e.g., price lists, business cards), or preparing your work for transportation.

3. Promote your participation: Promote your participation in the art fair or exhibition to your followers and potential buyers. This may involve sharing your art on social media, sending out newsletters or press releases, or creating promotional materials (e.g., postcards, flyers).

4. Engage with attendees: Engage with attendees at the art fair or exhibition. This may involve answering questions about your art, providing information about your process or style, or networking with other artists and gallerists.

Network with other artists and gallerists: Networking with other artists and gallerists can also help you get representation and build relationships with galleries. Attend gallery openings and artist talks, join artist organizations, and participate in online art communities to connect with other artists and gallerists. Here are a few tips for networking with other artists and gallerists:

1. Attend art fairs and exhibitions: Art fairs and exhibitions are great places to meet other artists and gallerists and showcase your work. Attend these events and take the opportunity to introduce yourself and your art to others.

2. Join artist organizations: Joining artist organizations is another way to network with other artists and gallerists. These organizations may host events, exhibitions, or artist talks, and provide opportunities to connect with others in the art community.

3. Participate in online art communities: Online art communities, such as forums, blogs, or social media groups, are another way to network with other artists and gallerists. Participate in these communities by sharing your art, commenting on others' work, and engaging with others.

4. Host your own events or exhibitions: Hosting your own events or exhibitions is another way to network with other artists and gallerists. By hosting your own exhibitions or events, you can showcase your art, meet potential buyers or collectors, and build your reputation as an artist.

By networking with other artists and gallerists, you can build relationships, learn from others, and promote your art.

* * *

Show your work in a professional manner: To get representation and work with galleries, it's important to show your work in a professional manner. This may involve creating a professional portfolio, framing your work, or presenting your work in a way that showcases your style and process. Here are a few tips for showing your work in a professional manner:

1. Create a professional portfolio: A professional portfolio is a key component of showing your work in a professional manner. Your portfolio should showcase your best work and give a sense of your style and process. Use high-quality images and present your work in a cohesive and visually appealing way.

2. Frame your work: If you are showing your work in person, consider framing your work to give it a professional appearance. Choose frames that complement your art and are appropriate for the type of work you are showing.

3. Use a professional website: A professional website is another important aspect of showing your work in a professional manner. Your website should showcase your art, provide information about your process and style, and include contact information.

4. Follow gallery submission guidelines: If you are submitting your work to galleries for consideration, be sure to follow their submission guidelines. This may include guidelines for the materials you need to submit (e.g., images, resume, statement), and the process for submitting your work.

Follow gallery submission guidelines: Many galleries have specific submission guidelines that you need to follow in order to get representation. These guidelines may include the types of art they represent, the materials you need to submit (e.g., images, resume, statement), and the process for submitting your work. Be sure to follow these guidelines carefully to increase your chances of getting representation. Here are a few tips for following gallery submission guidelines:

1. Read the guidelines carefully: Make sure to read the submission guidelines carefully and follow them exactly. This may include guidelines for the types of art the gallery represents, the materials you need to submit (e.g., images, resume, statement), and the process for submitting your work.

2. Tailor your submission to the gallery: Tailor your submission to the gallery by highlighting your art that aligns with the gallery's focus and mission. If the gallery represents artists in a specific medium, genre, or style, focus on showcasing your work that fits within these parameters.

3. Use high-quality images: Use high-quality images of your art in your submission. These images should be clear, well-lit, and accurately represent your art.

4. Follow the submission process: Follow the submission process exactly as outlined by the gallery. This may involve submitting your materials through an online form or email, or mailing them to the gallery. Be sure to follow all instructions and deadlines to increase your chances of getting representation.

Understand gallery contracts: If you do get representation, you'll need to understand the terms of your contract with the gallery. Gallery contracts can be complex, and it's important to understand your rights and responsibilities as an artist. Be sure to read and understand your contract before signing it, and consider seeking legal advice if you have any questions. Here are a few key points to consider when understanding gallery contracts:

1. Representation: The primary purpose of a gallery contract is to establish a relationship between you and the gallery, in which the gallery represents your art. This means that the gallery will promote your art, sell your art on your behalf, and provide you with a percentage of the sales.

2. Terms and duration: The contract should specify the terms of the representation, including the duration of the contract, the percentage of sales you will receive, and any exclusivity provisions.

3. Rights and responsibilities: The contract should also specify the rights and responsibilities of both you and the gallery. This may include provisions related to the promotion and sale of your art, the use of your images, and the handling of returns or exchanges.

4. Termination: The contract should also specify the conditions under which the contract can be terminated, such as breach of contract or failure to meet certain performance standards.

Build a relationship with the gallery: Building a relationship with the gallery is an important aspect of getting representation and working with galleries. This may involve working with the gallery to promote your art, attending gallery events, and staying in touch with the gallery staff. By building a good relationship with the gallery, you can increase your chances of success and build a sustainable career as an artist. Here are a few tips for building a relationship with the gallery:

1. Communicate regularly: Communicate regularly with the gallery staff to keep them informed about your art, exhibitions, and other updates. This may involve sending newsletters, updating your portfolio, or sharing your art on social media.

2. Attend gallery events: Attend gallery events, such as exhibitions, artist talks, and opening receptions, to support the gallery and build relationships with other artists and gallerists.

3. Promote your art: Work with the gallery to promote your art and exhibitions. This may involve creating marketing materials, such as press releases, social media posts, or emails, or participating in interviews or other promotional opportunities.

4. Be professional and responsive: Be professional and responsive when working with the gallery. This includes meeting deadlines, following through on commitments, and communicating clearly and effectively.

CHAPTER 8

Creating and Selling Art Licenses

In 'Creating and Selling Art Licenses,' learn the strategies and techniques for effectively licensing your art and generating income from your art. Discover how to research potential licensing partners, create a portfolio of your art, negotiate licensing agreements, and manage the rights and usage of your art.

This chapter will also cover how to identify potential licensing opportunities and how to approach potential licensing partners, as well as how to create a professional portfolio of your art. You'll also learn about the benefits of licensing your art, such as the ability to generate passive income and the opportunity to reach new audiences. By the end of this chapter, you'll have the tools and strategies you need to create and sell art licenses effectively, and to achieve financial success as an artist.

Creating and selling art licenses is a way for artists to monetize their art by allowing others to use their artwork for specific purposes.

Determine the rights you want to grant: When creating an art license, it's important to determine the rights you want to grant for your art. This may include the right to reproduce your art, the right to display your art publicly, or the right to use your art in a specific context (e.g., on a website, in a marketing campaign).

Create a license agreement: Once you have determined the rights you want to grant, create a license agreement that outlines the terms of the license. This agreement should include details such as the rights being granted, the duration of the license, the fee for the license, and any limitations or restrictions on use.

Determine the license fee: Determine the license fee for your art based on the rights being granted, the duration of the license, and the potential value of the art to the licensee. Consider factors such as the type of art, the size and resolution of the art, and the intended use of the art. You may want to research similar licenses and fees in your field to help guide your pricing.

Market and sell your art licenses: Once you have created your license agreement and determined your license fee, market and sell your art licenses to potential licensees. This may involve promoting your art and license offerings on your website or social media, or attending art fairs or exhibitions. You may also want to consider working with a licensing agent or representation to help market and sell your art licenses.

CHAPTER 9

Teaching Art Classes and Workshops

In 'Teaching Art Classes and Workshops,' learn the strategies and techniques for effectively teaching art classes and workshops, and generate income from your art. Discover how to determine your teaching style and focus, create a lesson plan, choose a location, promote your class or workshop, and engage with your students.

This chapter will also cover how to determine the appropriate pricing for your classes and workshops, and how to market your offerings to attract students. Additionally, you'll learn about the benefits of teaching art, such as the opportunity to share your skills and knowledge, and the chance to connect with other artists and art enthusiasts. By the end of this chapter, you'll have the tools and strategies you need to teach art classes and workshops effectively, and to achieve financial success as an artist.

Teaching art classes and workshops is a way for artists to share their skills and knowledge with others, and to create additional income streams. Here are a few tips for teaching art classes and workshops:

1. Determine your teaching style and focus: Determine your teaching style and focus. This may involve considering your strengths as an artist, the types of art you enjoy creating and teaching, and the types of students you want to teach.

2. Create a lesson plan: Create a lesson plan for your art class or workshop. This should outline the objectives, materials, and activities for each lesson, and should be tailored to your students' skill level and interests.

3. Choose a location: Choose a location for your art class or workshop. This may be a studio, art school, community center, or other appropriate space. Consider factors such as availability, cost, and accessibility.

4. Promote your class or workshop: Promote your art class or workshop to potential students. This may involve creating flyers, posters, or social media posts, or promoting your class or workshop through your website or email list.

5. Engage with your students: Engage with your students during the art class or workshop. This may involve demonstrating techniques, answering questions, and providing feedback on their work.

By teaching art classes and workshops, you can share your skills and knowledge with others, and create additional income streams, which can help you build a successful and sustainable career as an artist.

* * *

In addition to the above tips, here are a few additional

considerations for teaching art classes and workshops:

1. Determine your fees: Determine your fees for your art class or workshop based on the length and content of the class, the materials provided, and the location and overhead costs. Consider factors such as your level of experience, your market, and the value of your class or workshop to your students.

2. Consider offering different formats: Consider offering different formats for your art class or workshop, such as in-person, online, or hybrid options. This can help you reach a wider range of students and accommodate different schedules and preferences.

3. Create a welcoming and inclusive environment: Create a welcoming and inclusive environment for your students, regardless of their skill level or experience. Encourage a sense of community and support among your students, and be open to feedback and suggestions.

4. Continuously improve and update your classes: Continuously improve and update your art classes and workshops to stay current and relevant. This may involve incorporating new techniques or materials, or incorporating feedback from your students.

By following these tips and considerations, you can effectively teach art classes and workshops and build a successful and sustainable career as an artist.

CHAPTER 10

Collaborating and Networking with Other Artists

In 'Collaborating and Networking with Other Artists,' learn the strategies and techniques for effectively collaborating and networking with other artists to grow your art business and achieve financial success. Discover how to build and maintain professional relationships, seek out collaboration opportunities, and network with other artists and art industry professionals.

This chapter will also cover how to identify potential collaboration partners and how to approach them, as well as how to negotiate terms and agreements for collaborations. You'll also learn about the benefits of collaborating and networking, such as the opportunity to learn from and support other artists, and the chance to expand your reach and gain new customers. By the end of this chapter, you'll have the tools and strategies you need to collaborate and network effectively, and to achieve financial success as an artist.

Collaborating and networking with other artists is a valuable way for artists to share ideas, resources, and support, and to build relationships in the art world. Here are a few tips for collaborating and networking with other artists:

Attend art events and exhibitions: One way to connect with other artists is to attend art events and exhibitions, such as gallery openings, artist talks, or art fairs. These events provide opportunities to meet other artists, learn about their work, and potentially establish connections and collaborations. When attending art events and exhibitions, be sure to introduce yourself to other artists, engage in conversations about their work, and exchange contact information.

Join art organizations and groups: Another way to connect with other artists is to join art organizations and groups, such as artist collectives, art associations, or artist networks. These groups can provide a sense of community and support, and can offer opportunities to participate in group exhibitions or events. Joining an art organization or group can also be a good way to learn about other artists and their work, and to get feedback on your own art.

Participate in artist residencies: Artist residencies are programs that provide artists with a dedicated space and time to create and collaborate with other artists. Participating in an artist residency can be a valuable opportunity to focus on your art, learn from other artists, and build relationships in the art world. There are many artist residencies available, with varying lengths, locations, and focus areas, so be sure to research and apply to programs that align with your interests and goals.

Collaborate on projects: Collaborating on projects with other artists can be a rewarding and enriching experience. Collaborations can take many forms, such as exhibitions, installations, or publications, and can help you learn from other artists and create new work that may not be possible individually. When collaborating on projects, be sure to communicate clearly with your collaborators, establish roles and responsibilities, and create a plan for the project.

Use social media and online platforms: Social media and online platforms, such as Instagram, Facebook, or LinkedIn, can be useful tools for connecting with other artists and sharing your work. These platforms can help you build an online presence and reach a wider audience, and can also be useful for finding opportunities, such as exhibitions or residencies. When using social media and online platforms, be sure to engage with other artists and share your work in a professional and respectful manner.

By collaborating and networking with other artists, you can share ideas, resources, and support, and build relationships in the art world, which can help you build a successful and sustainable career as an artist.

CHAPTER 11

Diversifying Your Income Streams

In 'Diversifying Your Income Streams,' learn the strategies and techniques for effectively diversifying your income streams as an artist to achieve financial stability and success. Discover how to identify and explore new income streams, such as teaching art classes and workshops, licensing your art, and creating and selling products featuring your art.

This chapter will also cover how to assess the potential of different income streams and how to prioritize your efforts, as well as how to manage multiple income streams effectively. You'll also learn about the benefits of diversifying your income streams, such as the ability to weather economic downturns and the freedom to pursue your art on your own terms. By the end of this chapter, you'll have the tools and strategies you need to diversify your income streams effectively, and to achieve financial success as an artist.

Diversifying your income streams is an important strategy for artists to build a sustainable and successful career. Here are a few tips for diversifying your income streams:

Sell your artwork: Selling your artwork is the most obvious way for artists to generate income, and can take many forms, such as selling original artworks, prints, or licensed products. To sell your artwork effectively, it is important to understand your target market, price your artwork competitively, and promote your art to potential buyers.

Teach art classes and workshops: Teaching art classes and workshops is another way for artists to generate income, by sharing their skills and knowledge with others. To teach art classes and workshops effectively, it is important to determine your teaching style and focus, create a lesson plan, choose a location, promote your class or workshop, and engage with your students.

Licensing your artwork: Licensing your artwork is a way for artists to generate income by allowing others to use their art for various purposes, such as in advertising, product packaging, or home decor. To license your artwork effectively, it is important to research potential licensing partners, create a portfolio of your art, negotiate licensing agreements, and manage the rights and usage of your art.

Create a business: Creating a business around your art is another way to diversify your income streams. This may involve selling art-related products, such as art supplies or merchandise, or offering art-related services, such as commission work or art consulting. To create a successful business, it is important to research your market, create a business plan, and manage your finances effectively.

Freelance or contract work: Freelance or contract work is another way for artists to diversify their income streams by offering their skills and expertise to clients on a project-by-project basis. Freelance or contract work may involve creating artwork for clients, teaching art classes or workshops, or offering art-related services, such as design or illustration. To succeed in freelance or contract work, it is important to build a portfolio of your work, establish your rates, and market yourself to potential clients.

By diversifying your income streams, you can build a sustainable and successful career as an artist, by generating multiple sources of income and reducing your reliance on any one revenue stream.

CHAPTER 12

Managing Your Finances and Staying Focused on Your Goals

In 'Managing Your Finances and Staying Focused on Your Goals,' learn the strategies and techniques for effectively managing your finances and staying focused on your goals as an artist. Discover how to create a budget, track your income and expenses, and set financial goals.

This chapter will also cover how to create a financial plan and how to review and adjust your budget regularly, as well as how to stay motivated and focused on your goals. You'll also learn about the importance of managing your finances and staying focused on your goals, such as the ability to achieve financial stability and success, and the freedom to pursue your art on your own terms. By the end of this chapter, you'll have the tools and strategies you need to manage your finances and stay focused on your goals effectively, and to achieve financial success as an artist.

Managing your finances and staying focused on your goals are important strategies for artists to build a sustainable and successful career.

Here are a few tips for managing your finances and staying focused on your goals:

Set financial goals: Setting financial goals is an important first step in managing your finances as an artist. These goals may include increasing your income, saving for a specific purpose, or reducing expenses. Setting financial goals can help you stay motivated and focused, and can provide a sense of accomplishment when you achieve them.

Create a budget: Creating a budget is an important tool for managing your finances and staying on track with your financial goals. A budget can help you track your income and expenses, and identify areas where you can save money. There are many budgeting tools and methods available, so choose the one that works best for you and your financial situation.

Track your income and expenses: Tracking your income and expenses is an important aspect of managing your finances. This may involve keeping receipts, recording your income and expenses in a spreadsheet or budgeting app, or using a financial tracking tool. By tracking your income and expenses, you can get a better understanding of your financial situation and identify areas where you can save or invest.

Seek financial advice: Seeking financial advice from a professional, such as a financial planner or accountant, can be a valuable resource for managing your finances as an artist. A financial advisor can help you create a budget, set financial goals, and make informed financial decisions.

Develop financial habits: Developing financial habits, such as saving a portion of your income, paying bills on time, and investing in your art business, can help you manage your finances effectively and stay focused on your goals. These habits can take time to develop, but they can be a valuable investment in your long-term financial success as an artist.

By managing your finances and staying focused on your goals, you can build a sustainable and successful career as an artist, by creating a solid financial foundation and staying motivated to achieve your goals.

www.ingramcontent.com/pod-product-compliance
Lightning Source LLC
Chambersburg PA
CBHW050254220526
45465CB00002B/674